THERE IS ALWAYS HOPE

My Story of Redemption & Transformation

by Bayless Conley

answers *with*
BAYLESS CONLEY

Answers with Bayless Conley
P.O. Box 417
Los Alamitos, CA 90720
answersbc.org

There Is Always Hope
My Story of Redemption
and Transformation

Published by DUNHAM+COMPANY PUBLISHING

©2005 by Bayless Conley
Published 2006

ISBN: 0-9787116-1-0

Unless otherwise noted,
all scripture quotations are taken
from the *NEW KING JAMES VERSION*.
Copyright © 1982 by Thomas Nelson, Inc.
Used by permission. All rights reserved.

Cover Design by: Michael Holter Creative

Printed in the United States of America
ALL RIGHTS RESERVED

No part of this publication may be reproduced, stored in a
retrieval system, or transmitted, in any form or by any means—
electronic, mechanical, photocopying, recording, or otherwise—
without prior written permission from the author.

For information:

DUNHAM+COMPANY PUBLISHING
15455 Dallas Parkway, Sixth Floor
Addison, Texas 75001
dunhambooks.com

Table of Contents

Introduction	1
The Early Years	3
Then the Drugs Started	5
My Family Life	15
My Religious Upbringing	17
On the Run	19
Jesus on My Mind	25
Family Restoration	45
Help for Hungry Hearts	51

There Is Always Hope

My Story of Redemption and Transformation

INTRODUCTION

My life is an amazing story of God's unfathomable grace. When I think of the depths to which I fell…and all the trouble I got myself into…it's a wonder I am even alive today!

Day after day, month after month, and year after year, I fell deeper into the abyss of drug and alcohol abuse. I was desperately searching for truth…for the meaning to my life…for any answer as to why I was here. But nothing satisfied. Nothing filled that empty void. And nothing gave me the answer I was looking for—until that day in 1975, when I was confronted with the truth by a courageous twelve-year-old boy. Through him, I met the living Christ…and my life was changed forever.

If today you find yourself searching

There Is Always Hope

for the meaning to your life...if you wonder why you are here...if you struggle to fill that empty void in your life, then I encourage you to read on. What you will discover is the story of a journey filled with drugs, alcohol, and the occult—ending in rescue by God's love and grace at my darkest hour.

It is a story of hope—eternal hope. A hope that can be yours today.

My Story of Redemption and Transformation

THE EARLY YEARS

The story of my childhood is a lot like that of many kids raised in the 1950s and '60s. I was born in the city of Long Beach, in southern California, and I was raised as a normal southern California kid.

I was into sports, especially baseball. But when I entered junior high school, my life began a slow descent. First, I started smoking cigarettes with some other kids because I thought it looked cool. And then I started to drink because I thought that looked cool too.

I can remember getting up in the morning as a thirteen-year-old kid, drinking, and then going to school drunk. I can also remember going to school at times with just a terrible hangover, which pretty much became the norm for my teenage years.

As time went on, I began to drink more heavily and do things I thought were

There Is Always Hope

cool—but so damaging to me personally.

At one time, I was a very good baseball player and, like a lot of kids my age, it was my dream to play professionally. So when I was in tenth grade, I tried out for high school baseball. After making the team, I had my head shaved, which was required in those days for anyone participating on a school team.

My Story of Redemption and Transformation

THEN THE DRUGS STARTED

Just before the season started, I was playing basketball and hurt my knee. I ended up having major surgery. That injury ended my sports career. In that moment, something happened to me. While I didn't realize it at the time, it was the next step in that downward spiral. An outward sign of that change was my decision not to cut my hair for the next seven years.

Shortly after that, I smoked pot for the first time. The first joint I smoked that evening, on my high school property, led to a whole lot of other drugs. I started to smoke hashish and take LSD, speed, and barbiturates, and occasionally I snorted cocaine.

On top of that, the drinking increased. In fact, I was drinking all the time. It was not uncommon for me to just ditch high

There Is Always Hope

school, leave for the day, and go get stoned. It basically became my way of life...partying, chasing girls, and getting stoned.

On top of that, the drinking increased.

About that time a friend, who lived up north in a little commune, began to invite me to spend time with him. I thought it was so cool, because I would hang out with all of these older guys for a couple days, buy drugs from them, and we would drink and just get high.

One day someone recommended a book to me about certain Native Americans who were searching for spiritual truth and breaking into the spirit realm through the use of drugs. He urged the use of "organic" drugs like peyote, jimson weed, and a bunch of other "natural" drugs.

I had already used a lot of these "organics," along with my normal "chemical drugs" and alcohol consumption. But with the encouragement of this new book, I began to favor the

My Story of Redemption and Transformation

organic drugs above all others (although I never stopped using other drugs or drinking). When I think of it now, it seems insane, but I used to sit in class after eating a bunch of jimson weed, hallucinating until I was barely able to function.

It may sound crazy, but even while I was using these drugs, I was earnestly on a spiritual trek, looking for the truth. Numerous times I would go out into the desert with a group of friends. We would find an isolated place to camp, and then all of us would get high and try to somehow get in touch with the spirit world.

It wasn't unusual for a dozen of us to be wandering around the desert after doing a bunch of jimson weed or eating a bunch of mushrooms or peyote. We would spend hours, in the middle of the night, wandering around a bunch of rocks, looking for

> **It may sound crazy, but even while I was using these drugs, I was earnestly on a spiritual trek, looking for the truth.**

There Is Always Hope

answers. It would be hilarious if it wasn't so sad—to think we would really find truth among a bunch of desert rocks!

But in my heart, I was crying out for the truth. I really was looking for something that would satisfy the emptiness I felt. And I can't tell you how many times, during the course of those years, that God spared my life. All I can say is somebody had to be praying somewhere!

> **But in my heart, I was crying out for the truth.**

For example, on more than one occasion, I passed out at the wheel of my car while driving, even on the freeway! I should have been another drunk-driving statistic, but somehow, miraculously, I was never hurt.

On another occasion, I went with a friend up into the mountains on one of our little spiritual treks. We had packed a bunch of organic drugs in our backpacks, along with quarts of beer. We didn't bring any food; we just brought beer. Once we got up in the mountains, we began drinking our beer and taking the drugs.

My Story of Redemption and Transformation

After getting pretty high, we started wandering around and found an old cave. It was a miner's cave.

This cave went into the heart of the mountain, and we began walking into it without thought of the consequences. We had a flashlight, which helped, but after about fifteen minutes, we started getting into water. We took off our shoes and kept going. After a while, we were trudging through almost waist-deep mud, with the water above it almost reaching our necks. I still shake my head in amazement when I realize that our noses were barely above the water and the roof of the cave was right over our heads. How we kept from drowning, I will never know.

How we kept from drowning, I will never know.

After what seemed like hours, we could finally see a little pinhole of light ahead of us. When we got to the source of the light, we had gone all the way through the mountain. When we emerged on the other side, we were covered with a sticky red

There Is Always Hope

mud and were utterly exhausted.

We definitely had not been in our right minds to do something so dangerous.

As if that wasn't insane enough, we turned around and went right back through the cave!

> **We definitely had not been in our right minds to do something so dangerous.**

There was another time I shouldn't have survived. It was at a place in the southern California mountains called Big Bear Lake. I was there with a bunch of friends…and again we had cases of beer and a load of chemicals.

The first night I drank about a dozen beers and smoked hashish. In my wisdom, I decided to walk out on the frozen lake at about one o'clock in the morning. Two other guys thought that was a really cool idea too. So we walked out into the middle of the lake where the ice ended, and just started grinning at each other. Then one of my friends started to jump up and down on the ice!

Within moments, he fell through the

My Story of Redemption and Transformation

ice...then I fell through, followed closely by my other friend. We tried desperately to get out of the bone-chilling water, but the ice would break and we would go under. We would try again, only to have the ice break again, and under we would go.

We started to panic, because this went on and on and on...and no matter what we did, we couldn't get out. We just plunged down into the water again and again. All of a sudden—I don't even remember how it happened—all three of us were lying on top of the ice!

We began laughing, as we headed back to the cabin to dry off and have some more beers. As I look back now, I truly believe angels pulled us out because somebody somewhere had a burden to pray for us. God very graciously spared our lives.

Over and over, I pushed the limits. It

All of a sudden—I don't even remember how it happened—all three of us were lying on top of the ice!

There Is Always Hope

became more and more obvious that my life was out of control. I was regularly taking several different kinds of drugs together, just trying somehow to kill the aching void I felt inside.

In fact, I remember one time in particular—I was probably around eighteen years old—when I started the night off by taking a hit of LSD. But that wasn't enough. So I went into my room, smoked some hash, and then came back out to watch some TV.

But that still wasn't enough, so I took another hit of LSD and went back to my room and smoked some more hash. After about thirty minutes, I went back to the hash pipe again—a short journey that I made about ten times that night.

Over and over, I pushed the limits.

At one point, I got up and went into the bathroom. As I was looking in the mirror, all of a sudden the whole room went "zooooom"…and seemed to shrink, along with me, down to miniature size. Right away, I knew I was in

My Story of Redemption and Transformation

trouble...and, in that instant, I started losing control.

I don't know if you will understand this or not, but I totally lost control of my emotions and my thoughts. And I started to hear voices. I ran into my bedroom, but the whole room was on fire—or so I thought—and those voices just kept getting louder. And there was this horrible screaming. I really thought I was in hell.

At that moment, this voice started saying, "You're going to be in an institution in a straitjacket, and this will never stop." I was terrified. Absolutely terrified. And at one point, I was so out of control that I took a large knife...ready to end my life. In fact, I came within moments of committing suicide.

> **I really thought I was in hell.**

That night I experienced what it may be like for a person to exist forever in hell. The Bible says a person who is eternally separated from God *loses* his soul. He has no control any more. This is exactly what I experienced that night. It was sheer terror and absolute torment.

I knew I was really in trouble and had to get out of the house, so I went out for a walk. The next thing I remember is becoming aware that I was down the street in a neighbor's yard. As I got up off their lawn, I had a mouthful of grass, and my hands were full of grass. I don't know for how long, but I had been eating the grass of the neighbor's lawn like a cow. You know you are not in good shape when that happens!

That night I swore I would never again in my life take LSD. Never. Other drugs were fine, just not LSD.

My Story of Redemption and Transformation

MY FAMILY LIFE

You might be wondering what kind of home I was raised in—and what was going on in my home when I got into drugs and alcohol.

To be perfectly honest, I lived in a normal home. My mom and dad were good people. They provided for the family. I can't slight them in any way. While they didn't know God, they were basically good parents.

But, I can say, there were broken hearts in my home because of my choices. My parents got calls from the high school about my behavior and all the things I was getting into. My mother cried herself to sleep night after night. As a teenager, there were times when I wouldn't come home for days, and my mom and dad had no idea where I was…or if I was alive or dead. If I did come home, it would be two

There Is Always Hope

or three o'clock in the morning. I would sleep until two o'clock in the afternoon, and then just start drinking and partying.

I remember coming home in the middle of the night and finding my mom crying. And it was obvious she had been crying for a long time. I think that's what really tore at my dad's heart the most—seeing what my lifestyle was doing to my mother.

My Story of Redemption and Transformation

MY RELIGIOUS UPBRINGING

I was raised in a Catholic church. My mom, my sister, and I attended fairly regularly, although my dad never went to any church.

The services were conducted in Latin, which made it very difficult to get anything out of it (unless you spoke Latin!). All of the time I attended, I never heard the gospel. I never heard that you could know Jesus and that He could change your life.

Finally, at the age of fourteen, I quit going to the Catholic church. Eventually, my mother and sister stopped going as well. It was then that my family started a search for spiritual truth. My mom got very involved in astrology and metaphysics. In fact, she got so involved that people came from all over southern California to have her do their astrology charts.

My parents started going to a

There Is Always Hope

metaphysical church, and I started reading the Bagavagita and going to a Hindu Temple in Los Angeles.

I became pretty intense in my search for truth. I checked out this religion...then I checked out that religion...then I would check out another. I even began going to channeling meetings where someone would supposedly be taken over by the spirit of some ancient master. That spirit would come into them, and they would speak and share this vast wisdom and knowledge. As I look back at it now, it is clear these people were possessed by demons.

> **I became pretty intense in my search for truth.**

That, along with everything else I explored, turned out to be a dead end.

ON THE RUN

I finally came to the point where I knew I had to get out of southern California. I was sure that if I stayed much longer, I would kill myself. I just couldn't live this way and live for very long.

So I decided to spend a year traveling around. I went to Utah for a while, and I spent some time in Arizona. I would work a job for a little while to get some money, and then I would party.

Finally, I went to my dad and said, "Dad, look, I'm going to try to go to college. Will you help me? I need to do something with my life, but I have to do it by getting out of southern California." I was really trying to turn over a new leaf.

I ended up at a college in southern Oregon. When I got

I was really trying to turn over a new leaf.

There Is Always Hope

there, I told myself, "Man, no more drugs. I'm just going to quit." I took some with me just in case though.

Walking across campus on the very first day, I ran into a drug dealer I had known while living in southern California. Right away he said, "Hey, Bayless, you want to get high?" And, of course, I thought that was a great idea, so we went and got stoned.

My resolution to turn over a new leaf quickly dissolved. The drug use intensified, the drinking only increased, and four or five nights a week I was drunk. This went on for years. It was not unusual for me to start my day with a fifth of tequila and have it finished by early afternoon.

My resolution to turn over a new leaf quickly dissolved.

All the while, I was still searching.

The new friends I met at college were not the best kind of friends I needed at that point in my life. I immediately found

My Story of Redemption and Transformation

myself back in the maze of drug abuse that I was trying to escape.

Remember when I flipped out that night on LSD, and said I would never take it again? Well, one year later—to the day—I "dropped acid" again. It was a kind of LSD that we called "window pane," and it was the same kind I had been using one year earlier.

> **All the while, I was still searching.**

This time, though, I took twice as much as I had taken the night I flipped out. We stayed up all night—never went to sleep. I was so "whacked out!" In fact, I remember sitting up the next morning in the back of my truck, looking out at a big mountain across the valley. I sat there for quite some time, watching herds of buffalo run all across the mountain.

The only problem was...there were no buffalo there. I enjoyed watching them anyway!

In the midst of this increasing abuse of drugs, deep in my heart I was really

There Is Always Hope

looking for the truth. And I was utterly frustrated. As I look back, I realize there is one significant lesson God has taught me. I learned we should never judge people by their outward actions, because we don't really know what is going on in their hearts. They may be crying out to God.

> **I learned we should never judge people by their outward actions, because we don't really know what is going on in their hearts.**

My use of organic drugs…and my search for truth, continued to intensify. During that one year in college, my life completely revolved around taking drugs, getting high, spending time with friends, chasing women, drinking, and taking courses like Eastern Mysticism and American Indian Religions.

At the same time, I started associating with some people who were practicing witchcraft. I met a man who everybody was afraid of. He was casting spells on

My Story of Redemption and Transformation

people, and manipulating and controlling them. We became good friends.

In my search for truth, I thought this might be the answer. But every time he had a girlfriend, it would be just a couple of months until she would slit her wrists and try to commit suicide. Those same spirits that operated in his life affected everyone else around him. It soon became clear that what he had I didn't want.

> **Things just got darker and darker...worse and worse.**

But more and more, I was attracting these kinds of people. Things just got darker and darker...worse and worse.

Amazingly, many people thought I had it together. They would come to me for answers all the time. They thought, "He's really into nature, he seems like he's so collected. He must be tuned in to some important spiritual truth." It's pretty unbelievable now, but people were coming to me for counseling all the time. They had no idea just how miserable and empty I was on the inside.

There Is Always Hope

My Story of Redemption and Transformation

JESUS ON MY MIND

Then, after one evening of hard drinking and drug consumption, I woke up the next morning extremely depressed. I was so depressed that I decided to take a walk in the park not too far from where I was staying. I couldn't get Jesus off my mind as I walked. It was almost like a broken record that kept playing over and over.

I tried to think about something else, but my mind just kept coming back to the name of Jesus. Now, you need to understand that I didn't really know who Jesus was. I thought He was an Eastern mystic…someone who had studied mysticism in the pyramids of Egypt. Seriously! Somebody had told me that He studied in the pyramids, and I believed it.

I thought I was, perhaps, Jesus Christ reincarnated…or Judas…or someone in-

There Is Always Hope

between the two. But no matter what I did, I couldn't stop thinking about Jesus. So finally—as I was walking along a trail—I stopped and said out loud, "Okay, I will think about Jesus."

> **But no matter what I did, I couldn't stop thinking about Jesus.**

I continued walking, and ended up in a children's playground. It seemed like there were hundreds of kids running in every direction.

Suddenly a little boy walked by me, hands in his pockets. He never even looked up. I guess he was maybe eleven or twelve years old, and looked like he was either American Indian or Mexican. There was something about this kid that really struck me, but I couldn't put my finger on it. I knew it was good and it was wholesome...and I knew it was something I didn't have in my life.

I watched him walk by. And then I literally got up on my tiptoes to watch him until he disappeared out of sight at the other end of the park. I thought, *What does he have? What does that boy have*

My Story of Redemption and Transformation

that I don't? I just shook my head and went back to thinking about Jesus.

I walked on the trail for another quarter mile, went down a steep bank to a secluded area where no one could see me, and found a place next to the creek. I sat on a big rock and started throwing sticks into the water as I continued thinking about Jesus. About ten minutes later, I heard something, and looked up to see this same little boy sliding down the opposite creek bank on his rear end. He sat on a rock right across from me…no farther than ten feet or so.

He looked at me and said, "Hi," but I didn't answer him. Now, you have to imagine this scene. There I was with hair down past my shoulders, a long red beard, pants that had holes with my boxer shorts hanging out of them, and ripped-up elbows on the sleeves of my shirt—that was standard garb for me in those days. And here is this twelve-year-old boy trying

What does he have? What does that boy have that I don't?

There Is Always Hope

to engage me in conversation, and all I can think about is Jesus.

After he said, "Hi," he looked up at me, picked up a stick, and threw it into the water close to where I was sitting. There was this sort of silent communication going on. And then he broke it, by asking a question that nearly gave me a heart attack. Quietly he asked, "Do you know Jesus?"

And here is this twelve-year-old boy trying to engage me in conversation, and all I can think about is Jesus.

I about fell off my rock when he said that! My first thought was, *This kid thinks I'm Jesus.* I really thought that! I told him to come over to my rock, and he jumped across the creek and sat down next to me. His first words to me were, "Isn't He wonderful?"

For the next twenty minutes, this little twelve year old did nothing but talk about Jesus. He talked about Him like they were best friends. I had never heard anyone talk that way in all of my life—and I felt like I

My Story of Redemption and Transformation

was listening to a wise old man who knew so much while I knew so little.

Finally he said, "Come on. I want you to meet my mom." We got up, and I followed him across the park. We came to two little girls playing in the grass and a lady asleep in the grass. When we approached, she woke up sort of wild eyed—I can still remember the patterns of the grass imprinted on her cheek. Her son was standing there with a big smile on his face as if to say, "Look what I found!"— referring to me.

> **He talked about Him like they were best friends.**

I thought she was really nice, so I talked to her for a little while. Finally she said, "Bay—my nickname back then— come to our house for dinner." I said, "Lady, I don't even know you. I don't think so." She said, "Really, I want you to come to our house for dinner." But I refused and started walking away. As I was leaving, she told me her address. I just walked away and thought, *Strange day,*

There Is Always Hope

strange people.

About two weeks later, something told me I needed to find that house. I suddenly had this overwhelming desire—I didn't know where it came from—to visit these people. I remembered the address, so I got into my little pickup truck and found the street. I parked my truck and started walking down the street, looking for the address. All of a sudden, I heard someone calling from a second-story window, "Bay, oh Bay, over here." I looked up at her, and couldn't believe that she had seen me.

> **I suddenly had this overwhelming desire—I didn't know where it came from—to visit these people.**

When I got to her house, I realized they had dinner ready. And they had a place set for me. I said, "You knew I was coming?" They said, "Yeah. The Lord told us you would be here today, so we've been waiting." I said, "*Who* told you?" She said, "Jesus told us you would be here tonight, so I've had dinner ready,

My Story of Redemption and Transformation

and we've been waiting for about the last half hour or so for you to arrive. We knew you would be here."

Now, I used to have this habit of latching onto somebody's eyes when I talked to them. I would go eyeball to eyeball with them, and I wouldn't let go. I would get right in someone's face—invading their "comfort zone"—because I really was looking for the truth. I had learned that you can tell a lot by looking into someone's eyes.

> **And she just stared right back at me.**

So, at that moment, I got right in her face and said, "Who told you I was coming?" And she said, "Jesus." And she just stared right back at me.

I sat down to dinner, and for the entire evening, this Christian lady, named Ramona, and her kids talked to me about Jesus. The first time I ever heard the gospel was that day in the park…and then that night at their house.

After a long evening together, I still

There Is Always Hope

wasn't convinced this was the truth I had been looking for. I had to think about it, which I did. But I still continued doing drugs and drinking all the time. My life was still out of control.

> **My life was still out of control.**

In fact, there was one pretty scary incident that took place several weeks after my dinner at Ramona's house. I was hanging out one day with some friends, when a girl I knew showed up with a bunch of "magic mushrooms." She had been up in another part of Oregon, picking the mushrooms, which were extremely hallucinogenic.

She brought me an envelope full of these mushrooms. Now, I had been doing those for years, and I knew how much you could take. And in that envelope, there was enough for about ten people to "trip out" on. True to form, I ate all of them myself.

A little while later, at the house with my friends, things began to get really, really weird all of a sudden. The mushrooms I had taken hit me like a tidal wave, and I knew I had to get out of

My Story of Redemption and Transformation

there. My friends could tell something was wrong, so they wanted to know where I was going. I just told them I had to leave.

I figured that if I went to the park and just sat down for a while, everything would be okay. Well, I went to the park, but I was hallucinating, and things kept getting worse. In fact, they were so bad that I tried to just close my eyes…but that only made things more frightening. No matter what I did, it was bad! It was one of those times when I had absolutely no control. It was such a sorry state for a human being to be in!

It was a pretty pitiful sight as I walked down the street…so terrified by what I was seeing with my eyes open and terrified by what I was seeing with them shut. I decided to walk down the street with my eyes squinted, not quite shut and not quite open. It was still really awful!

> **It was one of those times when I had absolutely no control. It was such a sorry state for a human being to be in!**

There Is Always Hope

Somehow I made it through the night. How? I really don't know.

After that night, things went progressively downhill. I didn't see much of Ramona and her kids, and I began to hang out more with a friend of mine who was born in Mexico City. He became my best friend while we were in college.

Eventually I went down to Mexico with him to stay with his family. When we got there, I was blown away—it turned out that his father was very wealthy. An entire floor of a large apartment building was their home.

It was truly unbelievable. I had never lived in such luxury. Many of his friends were from the elite families of Mexico City, and so I found myself in the company of many rich kids. I remember one party we went to at what I can only call a mansion. As we walked down a long hallway, I saw many enormous rooms—some that would seat scores of people at elaborately decorated

> **Somehow I made it through the night.**

My Story of Redemption and Transformation

tables, and others that were used for entertaining guests—most of which, I think, no one ever used. The hallway emptied into a huge, domed room with elegant chandeliers, a pool table, sofas, and, oh yes…a giant swimming pool that was halfway surrounded with birdcages built into the walls. I'd never seen anything like it.

> **It was truly unbelievable. I had never lived in such luxury.**

My time in Mexico was really a time of extremes for me. On the one hand, there were lots of girls and no shortage of money. On the other hand, we would go out into the mountains and stay in poor Indian villages, and we would buy mushrooms and organic drugs from the Indians.

Those were the kind of extremes that were my life's dream. At one moment, I could be running around with girls and all these fancy people…and in another moment, I got the organic drugs and the spiritual dimension I searched for in nature.

There was one village in particular, called San Pedro, that had a little church.

There Is Always Hope

But it was a mushroom church. Guys would take mushrooms and sit in the church, with candles burning, and get visions. One day we went out to the end of the town with the mayor's daughter (we were buying our drugs from her husband) to a tiny shack that was maybe 20'x 20'. The mayor joined us, and we began to drink a local alcoholic drink called pulque, and we bought some mushrooms.

> **Those were the kind of extremes that were my life's dream.**

The next day, the shack was jammed with people, and when they saw me, several people said, "You've been here before." I'll never forget it. "You've been here before." It's like "whoo-oo-oo!!!" They told me that my spirit had traveled there before…and, of course, I was eating it up. You know, the devil will fill you with pride as long as you believe lies.

It was like a dream come true for me to be able to hang out with all these super rich people and drink expensive liquor, have the

My Story of Redemption and Transformation

finest pot that Mexico had to offer, and then go out to the mountains and get high... as I associated with the local Indians.

But I was so miserable. I was so empty. And I was being attacked in my mind by spiritual forces. I learned the hard way that when you do drugs like that, you open yourself up to the spirit world—and it is real! I began having experiences that I didn't like too much, and it finally got to the point that I wasn't much fun to be around. In fact, my best friend began to hope I would go away.

I can still remember sitting up every night on the elevated floor of that apartment building, opening the curtains, and looking for hours over all of Mexico City. I would sit there by myself every night, drinking a bottle of wine and looking out over the lights, thinking,

> **You know, the devil will fill you with pride as long as you believe lies.**

"There's got to be more to life than this. What's the answer?" I learned later that Ramona and her family were praying for

There Is Always Hope

me during that time. Even though they didn't know where I was, they faithfully prayed for my salvation.

One night, as I sat looking at the lights, the thought suddenly struck me, "I've got to get out of here." So I told my friend that I was going to leave and go back to Oregon.

Within hours, I had packed my little pickup truck and started my drive back to Oregon. I took one six-hour break to rest and stopped a couple other times, but I was determined to get back as quickly as possible. I didn't even really take time to eat. Of course, I did drink beer all the way back.

When I arrived, I just had to find Ramona and her family as quickly as possible. I found out they went to a Pentecostal church, so I drove there immediately. When I walked in the back of the church that evening, the twelve-year-old boy,

> **Even though they didn't know where I was, they faithfully prayed for my salvation.**

My Story of Redemption and Transformation

named Guy, saw me and came running back to me. He gave me a huge hug!

From that night on, I began to spend more and more time with them, and I learned about Jesus. I had been on a search for years…a search for truth. I had gone to the Mormon church, visited Hindu temples, spent time at metaphysical churches, and gotten into Yoga. I had been searching for truth through the use of drugs…trying to get outside of my body to experience true spirituality. I had done everything I could think of—but the very last thing on my list was Jesus and Christianity. I just thought that was for wimps. In my search for truth, Jesus was absolutely dead last on the list of the things I wanted to look into.

But, as I began to weigh what I was hearing from Ramona and her family with all the religions and spiritual stuff I had

There Is Always Hope

investigated, it became clear to me that Jesus was who He said He was. I even started telling my friends, "You know, I think Jesus is real. I think the gospel and this stuff they are telling me about Jesus is true. I really think He is the Son of God. I think He is it."

The people who I thought were my friends started persecuting me. They said, "Oh, how can you say that? What about the pygmies in Africa...are they going to hell? And are you saying that all of the Hari Krishnas are going to hell? You think your little Jesus is right?"

> You know, I think Jesus is real. I really think He is the Son of God. I think He is it.

I didn't have answers for them, but I knew something was happening to my heart. Man, was it ever a time of turmoil for me!

One night I was staying at a house with some friends when I decided to go outside. It was a cold night, not a cloud in the sky. I actually lay down on the hood of my pickup truck, and I started talking

My Story of Redemption and Transformation

to God. After a while, I even began yelling at God, "God, if Jesus is really Your Son—if this is true—You've got to show me. If it's true, what about this?" And I said something about the pygmies or something like that. Then I said, "If it's true, what about this, what about that?" And it was like heaven was silent, like brass above my head. I started to cry, and I said, "Forget it," and went into the house to go to sleep.

But the next day, something amazing happened. God talked to me. I don't know how I knew it, but I just knew it was God. He said, "I want you to go to Ramona's house." So I got in my truck and drove to her house. When I got there, they were packing everything up and getting ready to leave. Seeing them about to leave, I doubted what I had heard, and thought, *Oh sure, that was God telling me to come here!*

So I asked them where they were going. They said, "Well, we're going to Medford

But the next day, something amazing happened. God talked to me.

41

There Is Always Hope

to a mission there. We're going to share the gospel with street people, derelicts, and alcoholics." And God spoke to me again, and He said to me as clearly as I've ever heard any voice in my life, "I want you to go with them."

> **Now, this was the second time I had ever heard God speak to me in my life, and I argued with Him.**

Now, this was the second time I had ever heard God speak to me in my life, and I argued with Him. In my heart, I said, "I don't want to. I tell you what...I'll make You a deal. If they invite me, I'll go." Just as soon as I had that thought, Ramona whirled around and said, "Bay, come with us." I said, "All right, I'll go."

When we got to the mission, I sat on the front row with all the street people. I looked a little odd with my sweatshirt, skin-tight, bright orange pants with big yellow stripes down the side, and a pair of boots. I sat on the front row with the attitude, *All right, bless me if You can.*

They began with something I had

My Story of Redemption and Transformation

never heard of before, a thing called testimonies. The first person up was a lady. She quoted the first question I had asked God the night before, as I lay on my pickup truck, and then shared the answer from the Bible. Next, a man got up and quoted almost verbatim the next question I had shouted at God from my pickup truck. He proceeded to share the answer from the Bible.

Three or four people got up after that, and every one of them quoted the questions I had shouted at God the night before. By this time, I realized God had set me up. All of a sudden, I began weeping and sobbing as I sat there on the front row, thinking, *My God, this is real.* I was weeping uncontrollably for about thirty minutes…I just couldn't stop crying. I suddenly realized that the God of heaven was interested in me. He had arranged that whole evening just for me.

That night I gave my heart to Jesus

There Is Always Hope

Christ, and since that night, I have never put another drug in my body. I was set free by the power of God in that moment.

> **I suddenly realized that the God of heaven was interested in me.**

Now, I have to admit that I still drank for about two weeks, but slowly I lost my desire for alcohol. And one day, while sitting behind The Cheshire Cat, a little store that sold imported beer and wine, I had a remarkable experience. I had purchased a six-pack of imported German beer, which I fully intended on finishing off. But as I started drinking my second beer, I suddenly said, "I don't need this any more." I poured it and the remaining four bottles in the trash. Then I went home and poured the alcohol I had there down the toilet. From that moment, I was set free from the power of alcohol.

After being an alcoholic for so many years—and after having a major league problem with drugs for most of my teen and early adult years—God miraculously delivered me.

My Story of Redemption and Transformation

FAMILY RESTORATION

Coming to faith in Jesus Christ changed my life in more ways than one. In Jesus Christ, I found the answer I had been looking for—but at the same time, it brought a lot of persecution. I lost about half my friends—the other half got saved—because I just didn't compromise. I made it clear to my friends that I was going on with Jesus. I didn't care who it separated me from or identified me with. I had spent a lifetime searching for this, and I wasn't going to be ashamed now.

> **In Jesus Christ, I found the answer I had been looking for.**

At least half of my good friends distanced themselves from me. I can remember walking down the street and seeing one of my closest friends coming toward me. When he saw me, he crossed to

There Is Always Hope

the other side of the street and pretended he didn't see me. And I lost my girlfriend. I had talked to her about going to church—and, in turn, she gave me an ultimatum, "Look, it's either me or this Jesus thing." So I said, "Bye-bye, honey." I was not going to give up Jesus for anybody.

When I came to Christ, I had been living above a bar. I had rented the room from a girl who was one of my old party friends. When I got saved, she kicked me out. She told me, "I can't have you around here any more until this religious fanaticism is gone." So I was out on the street, but God took care of me.

> **I was not going to give up Jesus for anybody.**

I hadn't seen my family in four years. I had stepped on their hearts and hurt them so badly…just devastating any relationship that was there. Things weren't right between us. What I didn't know was that my mother had been saved just after I became a Christian—and God wanted to make things right.

One night at a Full Gospel

My Story of Redemption and Transformation

Businessmen's meeting, I saw an elderly couple that I knew, Fred and Eva. Eva had known the Lord since she was a tiny little girl. She had walked with God for more than 60 years, and I so respected her. When I walked over to Eva to say "Hi," she grabbed my hand and started to prophesy to me. She knew nothing about my family situation, but she said, "Things are not right between you and your family. You've got to go home. God says you have to go home. You've got to go home!"

> **What I didn't know was that my mother had been saved just after I became a Christian — and God wanted to make things right.**

It was like God's presence fell on me out of heaven, and I began shivering like a leaf. So a couple days later, I sold a guitar. I had to get some gas money to get home (I was driving a little '63 microbus at the time…cool hippie car!). Before I left, I called my mom. I honestly didn't know if she would want me to come home or not. I

There Is Always Hope

dialed the number with fear and trembling. She answered, and I said, "Hi, Mom, it's me," and I asked her if it would be okay if I came home. She started to cry...because God had also spoken to her.

Later I found out that the same evening Eva had prophesied to me, my mother had been at a meeting when a young preacher stopped in the middle of his message and said, "There's a mother here. You haven't seen your son in four years. He's been involved in alcohol and drugs, and then he got into worse things, but his life has been turned around. God wants you to know He's sending him home, and it's done in the Spirit right now."

> **She started to cry...because God had also spoken to her.**

My mom told me that she elbowed the lady sitting next to her and said, "That's my son. That's my son!" When she got home, she told my dad, and his doubtful reply was, "It would take a miracle." And God did it!

My Story of Redemption and Transformation

A few days later, I rolled up in the driveway in that old '63 microbus, and God restored my family. My mother and father are now members of my church, and my sister and her husband are serving with us in ministry.

There Is Always Hope

My Story of Redemption and Transformation

HELP FOR HUNGRY HEARTS

I can say that God has been good to me. He answered the cry of my hungry heart. I truly believe God will move heaven and earth to get to someone who really wants to know the truth. There are a lot of people who say they want to know the truth, but they really don't. But if you are someone today who has a heart to know the truth, then I don't believe you have read this booklet by accident. You have read it by design…God's design. My life is a testimony to the truth that God is a miracle-working God. He *can* and *will* save you.

> **My life is a testimony to the truth that God is a miracle-working God. He *can* and *will* save you.**

You may be involved in drugs like I was. You may be enslaved to alcohol like

There Is Always Hope

I was. You may be deeply involved in sexual sins. You may be a husband who is cheating on your wife…or a wife who is cheating on your husband. Or you may be a very respected member of the community, with all of the outward trappings of decency and success, but inwardly you are bankrupt. And there is a deep longing in your heart to know why you are here and what happens when you depart this life.

The Bible says, "God so loved the world that He gave His only begotten Son, that whoever believes in Him should not perish but have everlasting life" (John 3:16). The truth is, people just like you and me have become separated from God because of sin, and there is an empty place within each of us. You could call it a God-shaped hole in our hearts.

> "God so loved the world that He gave His only begotten Son, that whoever believes in Him should not perish but have everlasting life."

My Story of Redemption and Transformation

The only thing that can fill that void is the person of Jesus Christ. I know. I tried every conceivable thing in this world to fill that void. But only Jesus made me whole. And He is eager to do that for you today.

If you have not accepted Jesus as your Savior, I encourage you to pray a prayer like this:

> *Dear Jesus, I know that I am a sinner and that I am lost without You. I believe You died for my sins on the cross and rose from the grave on the third day, and through Your sacrifice, You paid the penalty for all of my sins. I accept Your free gift of eternal life. Thank You for saving me. Amen.*

The only thing that can fill that void is the person of Jesus Christ.

If you prayed that prayer from your heart, know today that you are a child of God. I encourage you to seek out a Bible-believing church. And may God bless you as you walk with Him each day.

There Is Always Hope

My Story of Redemption and Transformation

About the Author

Bayless Conley grew up in southern California, where he became involved in a lifestyle of drug and alcohol abuse as a teenager. After years of searching for truth, and a number of near-death experiences, he found Jesus as his Savior when a twelve-year-old boy shared the gospel with him.

Today, Bayless pastors Cottonwood Christian Center, a thriving church located in Orange County, California. Known for his simple, straightforward, and practical presentation of the gospel, Bayless is a frequent speaker at Christian conferences around the world. His television program, *Answers with Bayless Conley,* is broadcast worldwide, airing in more than 100 nations. Consistently fresh insights make his proclamation of God's Word powerfully relevant to everyday lives.

Bayless and his wife, Janet, are the parents of three grown children, Harrison, Rebekah, and Spencer. Together they passionately pursue life, family, ministry, and their relationship with Jesus Christ.

There Is Always Hope

My Story of Redemption and Transformation

If you would like to know more about
additional resources from Bayless Conley,
or if we can pray for you,
please contact us at:

Answers with Bayless Conley
Post Office Box 417
Los Alamitos, CA 90720

answersBC.org

There Is Always Hope

My Story of Redemption and Transformation

There Is Always Hope